QUEENS OF THE ANIMAL UNIVERSE

AFRICAN LIONESSES

Hunters of the Pride

by Jaclyn Jaycox

PEBBLE
a capstone imprint

Published by Pebble, an imprint of Capstone
1710 Roe Crest Drive,
North Mankato, Minnesota 56003
capstonepub.com

Library of Congress Cataloging-in-Publication Data
Names: Jaycox, Jaclyn, 1983- author.
Title: African lionesses : hunters of the pride / by Jaclyn Jaycox.
Description: North Mankato, Minnesota : Pebble, [2023] | Series: Queens of the animal universe | Includes bibliographical references and index. | Audience: Ages 5-8 | Audience: Grades K-1 | Summary: "Lions are called "king of beasts." But a pride is made of mainly females. These mighty beasts hunt and bring back food for the whole pride. The group also depends on the females to care for young. Take a close look at African lions and the important roles lionesses play to ensure a pride's survival"-- Provided by publisher.
Identifiers: LCCN 2021054292 (print) | LCCN 2021054293 (ebook) | ISBN 9781666343038 (hardcover) | ISBN 9781666343090 (paperback) | ISBN 9781666343151 (pdf) | ISBN 9781666343274 (kindle edition)
Subjects: LCSH: Lion--Behavior--Juvenile literature. | Social hierarchy in animals--Juvenile literature. | Social behavior in animals--Juvenile literature. | Animal societies--Juvenile literature.
Classification: LCC QL737.C23 J3855 2023 (print) | LCC QL737.C23 (ebook) | DDC 599.75715--dc23/eng/20211122
LC record available at https://lccn.loc.gov/2021054292
LC ebook record available at https://lccn.loc.gov/2021054293

Editorial Credits
Editor: Carrie Sheely; Designer: Bobbie Nuytten; Media Researcher: Morgan Walters; Production Specialist: Polly Fisher

Image Credits
Capstone Press, 7; Shutterstock: BrightRainbow, (dots background) design element, Daniel Lamborn, 9, Dennis W Donohue, 11, Elmari Viljoen, 13, evenfh, 25, H. van der Winden, 29, Henrico Muller, 15, huang jenhung, 21, Jez Bennett, 5, JordiStock, 24, MattiaATH, 28, Mogens Trolle, 23, oNabby, 8, Ondrej Prosicky, Cover, Ozkan Ozmen, 19, R. Maximiliane, 27, Rostislav Stach, 12, Stu Porter, 6, Tony Campbell, 17, WinWin artlab, (crowns) design element

All internet sites appearing in back matter were available and accurate when this book was sent to press.

Table of Contents

Words in **bold** are in the glossary.

Lionesses Rule!

African lions are called the "king of beasts." They are known for being strong and powerful. People may think of male lions when they hear this. But female lions are rulers too!

Lionesses run their family groups, or prides. Let's learn more about these animal queens.

Lionesses are strong, brave leaders.

Meet the African Lion

Lions are in the big cat family. They are the second largest cats in the world. Only tigers are bigger.

African lions are **mammals**. Mammals have hair and breathe air. Baby mammals drink milk from their mothers.

Lion cubs drink milk from their mother.

African lions once lived across Africa. They also roamed parts of Asia and Europe. Today, they are found only south of the Sahara Desert in Africa.

Only about 20,000 African lions are left in the wild. Their numbers are going down. They are at risk of becoming **extinct**.

Lions rest in shade under a tree.

African lions often live in grasslands and open woodlands. Lions don't make shelters. They escape the heat by finding shade under trees. Females find dens before they have young. The dens help keep the growing cubs safe.

African lions spend most of the day resting and sleeping. They usually hunt at night.

Adult lions are top **predators**. No other animals hunt them. African lions hunt zebras and wildebeests. They eat impalas, gazelles, and giraffes too. Sometimes they steal meat from other animals.

A lioness hunts gazelles.

Powerful Bodies

Lions are the only big cats where adult males and females look different. Both have light yellow, golden, silver-gray, or brown coats.

A male has a thick **mane** around its neck. Manes can be golden, red-brown, or black. Manes darken as lions get older.

A male lion and a lioness

Lions have a lot of **muscle**. This gives them strength for making attacks. They can weigh more than 500 pounds (227 kilograms). They can grow to be nearly 10 feet (3 meters) long. Males are larger than females.

A lioness uses her strength to take down a zebra.

The long canine teeth at the front of the mouth help lions tear meat.

Chomp! Lions have powerful jaws and sharp teeth. They use their jaws to grab onto and pull down **prey**.

Lion Prides

Roar! Chuff! Lions are **social** animals. They are the only kinds of cats that live in groups. A pride lives in its **territory**. Lions communicate with one another through sounds and body language.

Prides can have anywhere from three to 40 lions. Prides usually include just one to three males. Many female lions and their cubs make up the rest of the group.

Male lions sometimes fight. A male in search of a pride will fight to try to take another male's place. The males in a pride change over time. But the females remain.

A pride's territory usually includes water sources that the lions can use.

All in a Day's Work

A lioness relaxes under a tree. Her cubs are playing nearby. Suddenly, she snaps to attention. She spies a hyena through the tall grass.

The lioness springs into action. With a mighty roar, she chases the hyena away. The lioness has done her job. The danger is gone. She returns to her cubs.

One important job of a lioness is to keep the cubs safe. This is no easy job!

Lionesses protect their cubs from any danger.

African lions can **mate** any time of the year. The females give birth in dens. It's important they stay hidden. Many animals attack lion cubs.

A female usually has two to four cubs. Often, at least two females in a pride give birth around the same time. The cubs are born blind and helpless.

Spotted fur helps lion cubs blend into the surroundings and stay hidden from other animals.

Raising cubs is a lot of work! Female lions help each other. Mothers must leave their cubs to hunt. The lionesses take turns looking after cubs. They make sure the cubs stay close by and behave. A growl or swat from a lioness lets cubs know they better shape up!

Lionesses teach their young how to hunt. After about two years, the cubs are ready for life on their own.

The male lions protect the pride. But they don't help raise the cubs.

Lionesses and a group of cubs

A lioness sneaks up on a zebra. She takes off, and the chase is on! Lionesses do most of the hunting. They are smaller and thinner than males. These features make them much faster than males!

After the prey is killed, dinner is served! Males eat first. The lionesses are next. The cubs snack on the leftover scraps.

A lioness closes in on a zebra.

Teamwork

A herd of antelope quietly munches on grass. Female lions soon have them surrounded. Whoosh! The cats rush the group. They catch two antelope. Dinnertime!

Antelope are fast runners. Lionesses often get close before chasing them.

Female lions work together as a team. Many animals they eat are faster than them. Some are larger than the lions too. Working in a group gives them a better chance at catching prey. The more food they catch, the more they can feed the pride.

Lionesses may form large hunting groups.

A lioness has just eaten. Her cubs are safe nearby. She yawns and lays down to take a nap. Her work is done—for now!

Lionesses are important to their pride. They provide most of the meals. They raise and protect the young. Day after day, lionesses help their pride survive.

A lioness rests while
her cubs play.

Amazing African Lion Facts

African lions are great climbers! They often climb trees to see if prey is in the area.

A lion's roar is loud! It can be heard up to 5 miles (8 kilometers) away.

The spots on lion cubs fade as they grow.

The number of African lions has declined by more than 40 percent in the last 20 years.

Lions are the only cats with a tuft of fur on their tails.

Soft pads on a lion's feet help it move quietly when sneaking up on prey.

Lions often hunt during storms. This makes it harder for their prey to see or hear them.

Male lions can eat as much as 90 pounds (41 kg) of meat in a day.

Glossary

extinct (ik-STINGKT)—no longer existing

mammal (MAM-uhl)—a warm blooded animal that breathes air; mammals have hair or fur; female mammals feed milk to their young

mane (MAYN)—long, thick hair that grows on the head and neck of some animals

mate (MATE)—to join with another to produce young

muscle (MUHSS-uhl)—a tissue that is made of strong fibers; muscles can be tightened or relaxed to make the body move

predator (PRED-uh-tur)—an animal that hunts other animals for food

prey (PRAY)—an animal hunted by another animal for food

social (SOH-shuhl)—living in groups or packs

territory (TER-uh-tor-ee)—an area of land that an animal claims as its own to live in

Read More

Kortuem, Amy. *A Pride of Lions*. North Mankato, MN: Capstone, 2020.

Koster, Amy Sky. *Lions*. Washington, D.C.: National Geographic Kids, 2018.

Scally, Robert. *All About the African Lion*. Hallandale, FL: Mitchell Lane Publishers, 2019.

Internet Sites

National Geographic Kids: 10 Lion Facts!
natgeokids.com/uk/discover/animals/general-animals/10-lion-facts/

Rolling Hills Zoo: Big Cats
rollinghillszoo.org/big-cats

San Diego Zoo Wildlife Explorers: African Lion
sdzwildlifeexplorers.org/animals/african-lion

Index

Author Biography

Behind the Lens Photography

Jaclyn Jaycox is a children's book author and editor. When she's not writing, she loves reading and spending time with her family. She lives in southern Minnesota with her husband, two kids, and a spunky goldendoodle.